The Passover Experience

הגדה של פסח

A Messianic *Haggadah* for Passover

Copyright © 2024 by Daniel Goldstein
All rights reserved

Cover design and page layout: Liz Rabbah

ISBN: 979-888-03920-7-0
Originally printed in Jerusalem, Israel

A production of **Jewels of Judaism Publishing & Sabbath Hosting**
www.jewelsofjudaism.com
Email: info@jewelsofjudaism.com

Produced as a ministry tool for **Ner LeRaglai Jewish Ministries**
www.nerleraglai.com or www.psalm119105.org
Email: admin@nerleraglai.com

The Passover Experience

הגדה של פסח

A Messianic *Haggadah* for Passover

Daniel Goldstein

Jewels of Judaism Publishing
Jerusalem, Israel
www.jewelsofjudaism.com
Email: info@jewelsofjudaism.com

This Passover *Haggadah* is dedicated to the memory of my mother Sandra Goldstein Havey (1943 - 2020). My mother and I enjoyed many Passover Seders together and it was from her that I learned to appreciate and discover the spiritual significance of celebrating the yearly Feast of Passover and Unleavened Bread.

Contents

Acknowledgements

This *Haggadah* is the outcome of 3500 years of Jewish history, about 30 years of personal experience in leading Passover Seders, as well as the input and editing skills of several friends whom I want to acknowledge here.

I want to begin by thanking those from my online teaching class who volunteered their time to read the original manuscript and provide feedback. Paul Chrisman was one of the first to take my rough manuscript and provide numerous suggestions that greatly enhanced the flow of this book. Lauren Salamone provided very practical feedback and let me know when something was not being communicated clearly. Thomas White, President of Ner LeRaglai, provided excellent feedback regarding many of the details in the original manuscript which forced me to go back and reword several phrases. Paul and Heidi Krihak provided helpful feedback as the manuscript was being completed.

Finally, I want to thank Glenn and Sharon Green who are friends and board members of Ner LeRaglai. Glenn's skill as a songwriter provided much needed clarity to the text while adding ease to the overall flow of the manuscript. Sharon's attention to detail was very helpful in the final edit of the manuscript.

I am extremely grateful for the independent input and feedback from each of those listed above as well as the many others who have been praying for this *Haggadah* book project to be a success.

Daniel Goldstein
Executive Director at Ner LeRaglai Jewish Ministries
Jerusalem, Israel

Foreword

by Glenn & Sharon Green

In 2014 I was searching for somewhere that our group could celebrate Shabbat (The Sabbath evening meal) while in Israel. God had arranged so many other details. Surely He would take care of this. But as the plane took off my heart was heavy because every place had fallen through.

Later that week we went to a prayer room in Jerusalem. We were drawn to pray and prophesy over the group that had just finished leading worship and Daniel was with them. As we wrapped up, he asked if we had plans the next evening for Shabbat. It may be the most emotional response he's ever had to a Shabbat invitation. I was instantly in tears as I testified to God's goodness and we graciously accepted. Ten years later I'm honored to call Daniel a friend and brother.

Over the years Daniel has hosted us many times in his home for Shabbat. We've hiked the Negev. We've celebrated Passover together online. And he has visited us in our home. If we lived closer, Glenn and I agree that Daniel is a friend we would just hang out with. He is a man of character, a student, a teacher, and a lover of the Word. His study, prayer, and ear to hear the Holy Spirit result in solid teaching. In *The Passover Experience* Daniel shares age-old traditions in the *Haggadah* along with insights of how Yeshua is revealed in the Passover.

I bless you to encounter God as you celebrate *The Passover Experience*. May every celebration be an ongoing fulfillment of the one new man as we gather together around the world, Jew and Gentile, remembering how God brought us out of slavery. I pray

Yeshua will reveal himself to you in the breaking of the bread and that the Holy Spirit will pierce your heart with a supernatural love for Israel and the Jewish people. Shalom!

- *Sharon Green*

It's funny the way God works to bring people together... I still remember my wife, Sharon, coming home after a trip to Israel with members of our congregation's prayer ministry so excited to tell me about this guy they met at a prayer watch. Sharon and the group had all been praying for an encounter in the land to connect them deeper to the people and culture. Along came Daniel inviting them all to a Shabbat meal the following night at his home in Jerusalem. This was the beginning of a long and dear friendship leading to many Shabbat meals, visits in both Daniel's home in Israel and ours in the states, and ultimately our involvement as board members of Ner LeRaglai.

As a Christian songwriter and first-time author I was honored to put my editing skills to work in this Messianic *Haggadah*. Sharon and I have led and participated in many Seder meals over the years often commenting on the lack of Messianic focused resources. *The Passover Experience* is a perfect tool for families and Christian congregations wanting to connect both Jewish and Christian cultures. Daniel's intense passion for teaching is revealed through detailed explanations and thoughtful side notes while maintaining the richness of this ancient ritual. His years spent hosting Seder meals and digging for deeper truths have shed light on the Scriptures for us and many friends we have brought to his table.

In my years as a Worship Pastor I have met very few teachers gifted like Daniel with such dedication to the text, spiritual awareness, and devotion to connecting Christians of today with the Hebraic Root. I pray this book will inspire and lead you to new traditions around your table as you experience the heart of Yeshua.

- *Glenn F. Green*

Glenn & Sharon Green reside in Spring Branch, Texas and (together with Daniel Goldstein) they were both part of the original board of directors establishing **Ner LeRaglai Jewish Ministries** *as a nonprofit organization in 2020. Glenn currently serves as a worship pastor in a local Christian congregation in Texas and he continues to use his spiritual gifts as a songwriter and author. Sharon currently works full-time as a Technology Director and is a Certified Professional Coach. Sharon's spiritual gifting is in prophecy which she continues to exercise as an Emerging Prophet.*

Introduction

The Feast of Passover, together with the Feast of Unleavened Bread, is a unique biblical feast that is woven throughout the Scriptures bridging the Old and New Testaments of the Bible. Anyone can read about Passover in the Bible; however, it is only in the personal participation in this biblical feast that one will experience the full expression of Passover just as the disciples shared this special event with Yeshua (Jesus) 2000 years ago in what has become known as "The Last Supper."

According to the sovereign plan of Almighty God, the first Passover event gave birth to the nation of Israel from which came the appointed Messiah. At His miraculous conception, Yeshua literally took on flesh in the form of a human and later gave up His life to become the sacrificial Passover Lamb. Passover defines the Jewish people as a nation and it defines all those who believe in the Messiah as the Lamb of God, both Jew and Gentile. The story of Passover is the story of the Bible.

The Hebrew Language

This book has been created as a guide through a traditional Passover Seder, including its Messianic fulfillment. The Hebrew word סדר – *seder* simply means **order** and is used in this context to refer to the order of service. The book used during a Passover Seder is called a הגדה – *Haggadah* which is Hebrew for **the telling**. A Passover *Haggadah* tells the story of Passover and contains the order of service. This Passover *Haggadah* is considered Messianic because it combines the traditional elements of the Passover Seder together with the knowledge that Yeshua has come as the Messiah in fulfillment of the biblical prophecies.

Throughout this *Haggadah* I have chosen to use the original Hebrew name for Jesus which is ישוע – **Yeshua**. The name ישוע – **Yeshua** is simply a Hebrew word (in both Biblical and Modern Hebrew) meaning **salvation** (as a masculine noun), or possibly **The LORD is salvation** (as a shortened form of יהושע – **Yehoshua**). Either way, the name **Yeshua** is a continual reminder of who our Messiah is and what He so generously offers to everyone in the world: **eternal salvation**.

The various blessings throughout this *Haggadah* are written in Hebrew, in transliterated Hebrew (English letters representing the Hebrew sounds), and in the English translation. Feel free to use the English and Hebrew as you see fit taking into consideration what is most comfortable for you and for those around the table as you celebrate Passover.

The Setting & Theme of The Passover Seder

Passover is meant to be experienced with family and/or community. Passover is not designed to be experienced alone but there is also no exact group size in which Passover is to be observed.

Two key themes of Passover are **freedom** and **redemption**. The LORD brought the Israelites out from Egypt, where they were slaves, to be a people and a nation who are called by His Holy Name in order to worship Him (Ex. 19:1-6). It is in this context that we observe Passover each year: we remember that we are no longer slaves under an evil and oppressive ruler but called into freedom to be the people of God.

One practical way this combined theme of freedom and redemption is displayed at the Seder table is by sitting comfortably at the table and reclining to the left as each of the four cups of wine is consumed. This tradition of leaning to the left while drinking a glass of wine is done to emphasize that we are no longer slaves but we are a free people. Another practical way to display this theme of freedom and redemption is by serving one another around the table (e.g., pouring water and wine into your neighbor's cup).

Although the Passover *Haggadah* presents a rather straight-forward manner in which to celebrate the Passover, there is great flexibility in how a Passover Seder can be organized and how it is observed around the table. Please feel free to be creative in observing the Passover Seder and to make it practical for all who will participate. If you have young children who will be at your Passover celebration, it is especially important to have opportunities in which they can participate, activities in which they can engage, and readings which match their level and ability.

Being flexible and creative in your Passover Seder also includes the option to choose which parts of this *Haggadah* to emphasize and which parts you consider less important. You may even choose to skip certain sections of this *Haggadah* in order to tailor it for your specific group. The Passover Seder should be a fun and meaningful experience, not simply a religious obligation to observe.

Preparation for Passover

Preparation is an important part of any Passover Seder. In the days and weeks leading up to observing Passover, it is customary to thoroughly clean the home in order to remove all leavened items (e.g., crumbs of bread or any trace of leavened items that could potentially be in various rooms of the home). The concept of "spring cleaning" may very well have been adopted from this biblical practice of preparing for Passover.

Removal of All Leavened Items

The practice of removing all leavened items from the home is part of the biblical command in preparing for the Feasts of Passover and Unleavened Bread:

> **For seven days you shall eat unleavened bread, but on the first day you shall remove dough with yeast from your houses; for whoever eats anything with yeast from the first day until the seventh day, that person shall be cut off from Israel.** (Ex. 12:15 - NASB)

Taking this Scripture to heart, the Jewish people continue to observe the commandment of thoroughly cleaning their homes in the days and weeks before Passover begins. This annual, detailed cleaning culminates with a special ceremony on the morning of Passover to burn a symbolic amount of leavened items (a small amount of bread crumbs are gathered into a piece of paper and burned in a safe and contained place).

Practical & Spiritual Applications

Although believers in Yeshua are not bound to keep Passover according to the Old Testament Law, the process of cleaning out all leavened items from the home can add to the practical lessons learned from Passover. You might also consider keeping your home free from leavened items for an entire week. This is a family or community decision that is to be considered for the sake of the experience and not a law to be kept legalistically.

Spiritually, it is beneficial to understand the symbolism of leaven as sin and to reflect on your spiritual life, as we read in the New Testament:

> 6 **Your boasting is not good. Do you not know that a little leaven leavens the whole lump of dough?** 7 **Clean out the old leaven so that you may be a new lump, just as you are in fact unleavened. For Messiah our Passover also has been sacrificed.** 8 **Therefore let's celebrate the feast, not with old leaven, nor with the leaven of malice and wickedness, but with the unleavened bread of sincerity and truth.**
> (1 Cor. 5:6-8 - NASB)

In the days leading up to Passover it is a good practice to remember the holiness of God and repent from any sins (words or actions) that are not in keeping with God's holy standard. Our bodies are considered to be the temple of the

Holy Spirit (1 Cor. 6:19-20. 2 Cor. 6:16), which is to be free from sin and anything that would defile it.

Physical Preparations for Passover

The following checklist details the items and foods which are part of a traditional Passover observation. It is wise to be familiar with this checklist so that all of the needed items will be bought and prepared before the Passover Seder begins.

1. *Matzah* **(Unleavened Bread)**: Plenty of matzah should be made available for the Passover Seder. The total amount needed depends on the number of people in your home or community. A good rule of thumb is a minimum of 2-3 matzahs per person; however, it is generally wise to have plenty of matzah so that there is no lack on the Passover table. If matzah is not available, any type of unleavened bread or cracker can be used as a substitute.

2. **Wine and/or Grape Juice**: Sufficient for four glasses per person. (Wine is the standard and I will use the word wine throughout the *Haggadah*. Wine and grape juice are both considered "the fruit of the vine" and either one or both may be used depending on the preference of your family or community.)

3. **Bitter Herbs (A)**: Horseradish or some type of spicy condiment (it should be moderately spicy). Minimum amount: 1/4 teaspoon per person.

4. **Bitter Herbs (B)**: Romaine lettuce (cleaned and ready to eat). At least one leaf per person.

5. **Vegetable**: Typically a green vegetable like parsley or celery (cleaned and ready to eat). At least one piece per person.

6. **Hardboiled Eggs**: Suggested amount is one egg per person. Additionally, one brown or roasted white egg (so that the shell is browned) is needed for display on the Seder Plate. The eggs to be eaten can be any color (white or brown).

7. *Charoset*: A sweet mixture of apples, walnuts, dates, cinnamon, and grape juice. A typical recipe for *Charoset* is as follows: 4-5 apples (e.g., Gala), 4-5 dates (or 1/2 cup of date syrup), 1 cup of walnuts. These items are to be chopped fine and mixed together. Then add 1/2 cup of grape juice and some cinnamon and mix together. There are many recipes online. You are welcome to do a search and choose the recipe that best suits your taste. The choice of ingredients is flexible.

8. **Bone**: A lamb or chicken leg bone (preferably a roasted bone). This bone is used for a symbolic remembrance of the Passover sacrifice.

9. **Passover Seder Plate**: Passover Seder plates are available for purchase if you choose to buy one. It can be helpful to obtain a traditional Passover Seder plate. Otherwise, any plate can serve this purpose. The Passover Seder plate is used to display a sample portion of specific Passover foods as listed below. (**Note**: The display of Passover foods on the seder plate is separate from the larger portions that will be eaten during the Passover Seder):

   - A lamb or chicken bone
   - A roasted (brown) hard boiled egg
   - A piece of parsley or celery
   - A small portion of the Charoset

- A small portion of the bitter herbs (horseradish)
- A small leaf of romaine lettuce

10. **Bowl of Salt Water**: Typically, a small or medium-sized bowl is filled about halfway with water. A teaspoon of salt is added and mixed into the water.

11. **Large Bowl & Water Pitcher**: These are used for washing hands.

12. **Hand Towel**: Used for drying hands after washing.

13. **A Matzah Bag**: A three-layered matzah bag (cloth bag with three pockets) is used specifically for the Passover Seder. You may choose to buy one, make one, or simply use a clean, towel-sized piece of cloth to separate and cover the three whole pieces of matzah.

14. **Clean Piece of Fabric**: A small towel or any clean, placemat-sized piece of cloth is needed for wrapping and hiding the broken piece of matzah (the *Afikoman*).

15. **Redemption Money**: A small gift (e.g., a chocolate bar) or a token sum of money (e.g., $5, €5, or 20 shekels) is used for rewarding the child who finds the *Afikoman*.

16. **Wine Glasses**: Either wine glasses or special drinking glasses. One wine glass for each person at the table to be used for grape juice or wine.

17. **Regular Drinking Glasses**: One for each person at the table for water or other beverages.

18. **Plates & Utensils**: Appropriate eating utensils for this special occasion.

19. **Extra Place Setting**: There should be an extra place setting at the table for Elijah. A chair is to be left empty

in front of a full place setting on the table.

20. **Two Candles**: Candles can be of any size. Candlesticks or tea lights may be used. You may use either a set of two candles on each table or just one set of candles on a table in your home or in the event hall, depending on your specific situation.

21. **Main Meal**: A variety of foods including the main dish (beef, chicken, or fish) with side dishes of rice, potatoes, vegetables, and various salads. Traditional Passover dishes and recipes can be found online. No bread or leavened items should be included in this meal. For the sake of Jewish tradition and the biblical narrative, it is culturally appropriate to avoid pork or pork products for this meal.

22. **Dessert**: Any variety of unleavened items (e.g., coconut macaroons, matzah covered with melted butter and chocolate, seasonal fruit, etc…)

23. *Haggadah*: A Passover Seder book for each participant.

The Leader, Participants, & General Information

The Passover Seder is generally observed together as a family or as a community and there is always a designated leader to guide the group through this event. In a family, the leader is typically the father. In a Christian community the leader is typically a pastor, an elder, or a respected member of that community. The leader for the Passover Seder needs to be clearly identified before the event takes place.

The designated leader should be familiar with the *Haggadah* by preparing in advance to guide the others throughout the Passover Seder. The role of the leader includes inviting and

assigning the participants at the table to read or perform certain tasks as described in this *Haggadah*.

Note: All of the content in this Passover *Haggadah* is arranged to provide an in-depth experience of a traditional Passover Seder. To help navigate the various instructions and activities in this *Haggadah*, specific instructions are included for the "**Leader**" and for the "**Participants**" as marked throughout this book. Any phrase or sentence following "**Leader**" or "**Participants**" should be read aloud as written. Any information in parentheses "(-)" for "**Leader**" or "**Participants**" is included to provide instruction or guidance for the designated person or group. The majority of the content in this *Haggadah* will be read or guided by the "**Leader**."

There are also "**Highlighted Boxes**" throughout this book which are included to provide information and context. The "**Leader**" may choose to read aloud or not read aloud the information in the "**Highlighted Boxes**." It is highly recommended that the designated leader for the Passover Seder be intimately familiar with all the material in this book before the day of the event in order to have the best possible Passover experience.

Setting The Passover Table

Place the Passover Seder plate somewhere in the center of the table, as it contains a sample portion of the meaningful elements to be eaten during the Passover observation. The following picture illustrates how the foods of Passover are to be arranged on the plate with each corresponding meaning briefly explained.

The Seder plate elements are arranged clockwise starting at 12 o'clock:

1. *Chazeret* – חזרת – Romaine lettuce (a bitter herb representing slavery)

2. *Zeroa* – זרוע – Shank bone (representing the Passover lamb)

3. *Karpas* – כרפס – Parsley or celery (representing spring/new life)

4. *Maror* – מרור – Horseradish (a bitter herb representing slavery)

5. *Charoset* – חרוסת – Sweet apple mixture (representing both the mortar used in Egypt for building and the Jewish people)

6. *Beitzah* – ביצה – Roasted egg (representing the cycle of life by its round shape and the hope of a rebuilt Temple)

Additional items on the Passover table:

- **Matzah (Unleavened Bread)**: Plenty of matzah according to the number of guests.
- **Matzah Bag**: The matzah bag containing the three matzahs.
- **Wine (and/or grape juice)**

The 15 Stages of The *Haggadah*

The *Haggadah* tells the story of Passover and incorporates various traditions of eating, drinking, singing, and reading in order to take you through the entire Passover event. To ensure the Passover is covered as fully as possible, there are 15 stages of the *Haggadah* that bring you through the various aspects of the Passover together with Jewish tradition. The leader and all participants should read through the list of stages at the start of the Passover Seder in order to be familiar with the flow of the *Haggadah*. The 15 stages are:

1. *Kadesh* – קדש – **Sanctification (setting apart as holy)**
2. *Urechatz* – ורחץ – **Washing**
3. *Karpas* – כרפס – **A Vegetable (typically green)**
4. *Yachatz* – יחץ – **To Cut in Half**
5. *Magid* – מגיד – **The Telling**
6. *Rachtzah* – רחצה – **Washing**
7. *Motzi* – מוציא – **To Bring Forth**
8. *Matzah* – מצה – **Unleavened bread**
9. *Maror* – מרור – **Bitter Herbs**
10. *Korech* – כורך – **Sandwich**
11. *Shulchan Orek* – שולחן עורך – **The Set Table**
12. *Tzafoon* – צפון – **Hidden**
13. *Barek* – ברך – **Blessing**
14. *Hallel* – הלל – **Praise**
15. *Nirtzah* – נרצה – **Accepted**

Lighting The Candles

Before beginning the Passover Seder, it is tradition to light two candles accompanied by a blessing. This is typically performed by the wife or mother of the home but it can be done by anyone in the family or community. The following blessing is a Messianic adaptation of the traditional blessing that reflects the heart of God for us today with Yeshua at the center.

(Participant: *The woman of the home or someone else should be assigned to say this blessing and light the candles.*)

בָּרוּךְ אַתָּה יהוה אֱלֹהֵיתוּ מֶלֶךְ הָעוֹלָם, אֲשֶׁר קִדְּשָׁנוּ בְּיֵשׁוּעַ הַמָּשִׁיחַ וְצִוָּנוּ לִהְיוֹת אוֹר לְעוֹלָם:

Baruk Ata Adonai Eloheinu Melek Ha'Olam Asher Kidshanu Be'Yeshua HaMashiach VeTzivanu Lehiyot Or Le'Olam

Blessed are you, O LORD our God, King of the universe who sanctified us in Yeshua the Messiah and has commanded us to be light to the world.

The Passover Experience
A Messianic *Haggadah* for Passover

The Passover Seder officially begins here. Family and guests are welcomed to the table and everyone should have their own copy of the Passover *Haggadah*. The 15 stages of the *Haggadah* will guide those around the table through a traditional Passover Seder from a Messianic perspective. All the participants should be familiar with the 15 stages as listed on p. 28. Before beginning with stage one, The Four Cups of wine are introduced here to explain their meaning, which is central to the Passover Seder.

The Four Cups

Leader:

Four cups of wine will be poured and consumed at different times during the Passover Seder, as noted in the *Haggadah*. Each of the four cups is identified by a particular name:

1. **The First Cup → Cup of Sanctification**
2. **The Second Cup → Cup of Deliverance**
3. **The Third Cup → Cup of Redemption**
4. **The Fourth Cup → Cup of Praise (Ultimate Redemption)**

The names for these four cups are not arbitrary, but are taken from the following Scripture verses in Exodus chapter six. The four italicized phrases in these verses correspond to the names of the four cups of wine:

> 6 **Say, therefore, to the sons of Israel, "I am the LORD, and** *I will bring you out* **from under the burdens of the Egyptians, and** *I will deliver you* **from their bondage.** *I will also redeem you* **with an outstretched arm and with great judgments.** 7 **Then** *I will take you for My people,* **and I will be your God; and you shall know that I am the LORD your God, who brought you out from under the burdens of the Egyptians.** 8 **I will bring you to the land which I swore to give to Abraham, Isaac, and Jacob, and I will give it to you for a possession; I am the LORD."** (Ex. 6:6-8 - NASB1995)

The Scripture phrases according to their cups are:

1. **"I will bring you out" = Sanctification ➜ First Cup**
2. **"I will deliver you" = Deliverance ➜ Second Cup**
3. **"I will also redeem you" = Redemption ➜ Third Cup**
4. **"I will take you for My people" = Praise (Ultimate Redemption) ➜ Fourth Cup**

These sovereign acts of God on behalf of the people of Israel help to outline the story of Passover as we partake of the four cups throughout the *Haggadah*.

The *Haggadah* begins with stage one as detailed below, including the explanations and blessings which are directed by the leader. Participants will not drink the first cup of wine until after the third blessing, as noted in the text.

Stage One: *Kadesh* – קְדֵשׁ (Sanctification)

The First Cup: The Cup of Sanctification

<u>Leader</u>:

The first stage, *Kadesh*, sanctifies or sets apart this special Passover Feast as holy to the Lord. As we begin this Passover Seder, I invite you to follow along with me in your *Haggadah* book as I read the following blessings. Everyone's wine glass should be filled at this time in preparation for the first cup. After the blessings we will drink this cup together in agreement.

If Passover begins on a Friday evening with the first day of Unleavened Bread being the Sabbath, start the blessings here with Gen. 1:31-2:3. If Passover and the Feast of Unleavened Bread begin on any other day of the week, skip Gen. 1:31-2:3 and start the blessings from the next highlighted box.

(עברית)

וַיְהִי־עֶרֶב וַיְהִי־בֹקֶר יוֹם הַשִּׁשִּׁי:
וַיְכֻלּוּ הַשָּׁמַיִם וְהָאָרֶץ וְכָל־צְבָאָם:
וַיְכַל אֱלֹהִים בַּיּוֹם הַשְּׁבִיעִי מְלַאכְתּוֹ אֲשֶׁר עָשָׂה
וַיִּשְׁבֹּת בַּיּוֹם הַשְּׁבִיעִי מִכָּל־מְלַאכְתּוֹ אֲשֶׁר עָשָׂה:
וַיְבָרֶךְ אֱלֹהִים אֶת־יוֹם הַשְּׁבִיעִי וַיְקַדֵּשׁ אֹתוֹ
כִּי בוֹ שָׁבַת מִכָּל־מְלַאכְתּוֹ אֲשֶׁר־בָּרָא אֱלֹהִים לַעֲשׂוֹת:

סַבְרִי מָרָנָן וְרַבָּנָן וְרַבּוֹתַי:

(*Transliteration*)
Vayehi Erev Vayehi Boker, Yom Ha'shishi:
Vaychulu Hashamaim Veha'aretz Vechol Tze've'am:
Va'ye'chal Elohim Bayom Hashe'vi'ee
Melachto Asher Asa
Vayishbot Bayom Hashe'vi'ee Mikol
Melachto Asher Asa:
Vayevarech Elohim Et Yom Hashe'vi'ee Vayekadesh
OtoKi Vo Shavat Mikol Melachto
Asher Bara Elohim La'a'sot:

Leader: *Savrei Maranan*
Participants: *LaHayim*

(*English*)
**And there was evening and
there was morning, the sixth day.
Thus the heavens and the earth were completed, and
all their hosts. By the seventh day God completed His
work which He had done, and He rested on the seventh
day from all His work which He had done. Then God
blessed the seventh day and sanctified it, because in it**

He rested from all His work which God had created and made. (Gen. 1:31b-2:3 - NASB1995)

Leader: *Savrei Maranan* (Pay Attention!)
Participants: *LaHayim* (To Life!)

> If Passover begins on any other day of the week (not on the Sabbath), begin the blessings here.

Leader:

בָּרוּךְ אַתָּה יהוה אֱלֹהֵינוּ מֶלֶךְ הָעוֹלָם בּוֹרֵא פְּרִי הַגָּפֶן:

Baruk Ata Adonai Eloheinu Melek Ha'Olam Borei Pri Hagafen

Blessed are you, O LORD our God, King of the universe who creates the fruit of the vine.

Participants: Amen

Leader:
The second blessing is a traditional Jewish blessing that has been changed and adapted for the Messianic faith. (*This blessing is only provided in English.*)

> **Blessed are You, O LORD our God, King of the universe, who has chosen us to be His own people and sanctified us in Yeshua the Messiah. And You, O LORD our God, have lovingly given us Appointed Times for gladness, festivals and seasons for**

joy, this day of the Feast of Unleavened Bread, the season of our freedom, a holy convocation in memory of our Exodus from Egypt and our freedom from sin through the Messiah as the final Passover Lamb. (A traditional Passover blessing)

The third blessing is a general blessing thanking God for sustaining us in life and allowing us to celebrate another festival before Him.

(**Leader**: *Invite the participants to join in reciting this third blessing with you.*)

בָּרוּךְ אַתָּה יהוה אֱלֹהֵינוּ מֶלֶךְ הָעוֹלָם,
שֶׁהֶחֱיָנוּ וְקִיְּמָנוּ וְהִגִּיעָנוּ לַזְּמַן הַזֶּה:

Baruk Ata Adonai Eloheinu Melek Ha'Olam Sh'hechyanu Vekimanu Vehigianu Lezeman Hazeh.

Blessed are you, O LORD our God, King of the universe who has kept us alive, and sustained us, and has brought us to reach this season.

(**Participants**: *Drink the first cup of wine. After drinking the first cup, wine glasses should be refilled in preparation for the next cup.*)

Stage Two: *Urechatz* – ורחץ (Washing)

This act of washing hands at stage two is done before touching the food at the next

stage. This stage is not mandatory and I generally skip it. If anyone would like to wash their hands at this time, they should do so now. There is another handwashing later in the *Haggadah* at stage six that will be a more interactive and biblically connected act.

Stage Three: *Karpas* – כרפס (A Green Vegetable)

(**Participants**: *Take a sprig of parsley and dip it twice in the bowl of salt water. The sprig of parsley is to be held over your plate until after the blessing is read aloud and then it is eaten.*)

A green vegetable is used to represent the spring season and the salty water symbolizes the tears of slavery while the Israelites were in Egypt.

(**Leader**: *Invite the participants to join in reciting this blessing together with you.*)

בָּרוּךְ אַתָּה יהוה אֱלֹהֵינוּ מֶלֶךְ הָעוֹלָם בּוֹרֵא פְּרִי הָאֲדָמָה:

Baruk Ata Adonai Eloheinu Melek Ha'Olam
Borei Pri Ha'adamah

Blessed are you, O LORD our God, King of the universe who creates the fruit of the ground.

(**Participants**: *The parsley, which has been dipped twice in salt water, is now eaten by everyone at the table.*)

Stage Four: *Yachatz* – יחץ (To cut in half)

(**Leader**: *Pick up the matzah bag containing the three matzahs, remove the middle matzah of the three matzahs and break it in half. Wrap the larger of the two halves of the middle matzah in a separate cloth and return the smaller half to its place between the two matzahs in the matzah bag.*)

> The larger piece of broken matzah that is wrapped in the separate cloth is called the "**Afikoman**" and it is to be hidden somewhere in the room by the leader during stage five of the Passover Seder. The *Afikoman* will be brought back to the table toward the end of the *Haggadah*.

Tradition & The Bible

Leader:
What is the meaning of the three matzahs and the middle piece that is broken in two with one piece hidden away?

The tradition of three matzahs during the Passover Seder was added at some point in history but there is no single explanation for it. There are some who say that the three matzahs represent the forefathers of Israel: **Abraham**, **Isaac**, and **Jacob**. There are others who say that the three matzahs represent **the priests**, **the Levites**, and **the people of Israel**, symbolizing the spiritual unity of the nation of Israel. For those who believe in Yeshua as the Messiah, we can see a representation of the triunity of God: **The Father**, **The Son**, and **The Holy Spirit**.

Matzah bread is unleavened bread and has various symbolic meanings. As noted earlier, leaven is used to symbolize sin in the New Testament (1 Cor. 5:6-8) as it is something that affects the whole piece of dough once it is added.

Matzah bread is prepared and baked in a careful but hasty manner to keep the dough from rising. After water is added to the flour, it is quickly mixed, divided up into smaller portions, and flattened. It is then pierced through with a special tool with spikes making holes in the dough in order to keep the dough from puffing up, and then it is baked in an oven.

The outcome of making matzah in this manner produces a flat bread made without leaven that is pierced through and striped (as a result of the rows of holes made by the tool). The *Afikoman*, the middle piece which is broken in two and hidden away, also has clear symbolic markers of the death and burial of the Messiah who was beaten with stripes on His back, pierced through by the nails in His hands and feet, broken in two by His death, and hidden away in His burial.

The *Afikoman*

Leader:
There are two main theories regarding the origin of the word *Afikoman*:

1. **Afikoman**: A Greek word meaning dessert or that which comes after.
2. **Afikoman**: An Aramaic word (afiku-kaman) meaning "remove from before us". (Lau. p. 309)

Rabbi Israel Meir Lau explains the possible origins of the Aramaic understanding of *Afikoman* in the following quote from his book **Practical Judaism**:

In ancient times, little tables were brought in for each meal, to hold the food. At the end of the meal, these small tables would be removed, to be replaced with trays of sweet things for dessert. While the Temple existed, the last thing that one was required to eat at the seder table, was the Pesah (passover) lamb, so as to have the taste of it linger in one's mouth. Today, when we have neither the Temple nor the Paschal (passover) sacrifice, we have only one Torah commandment in regard to eating, and that is to eat matza. We therefore make sure that the last thing we eat will be matza, so that its taste can remain with us after the meal. (Lau. p. 309 [words in parentheses added for meaning])

Rabbi Lau provides a contextual understanding of the *Afikoman* in the quote above while defending a possible Aramaic origin of the word. Whether the origin of *Afikoman* is Greek or Aramaic, the manner in which *Afikoman* is used in the Passover Seder is identical: it is used for that broken piece of matzah that is hidden away at the beginning of the Passover Seder and brought back at the end. It is both that which is removed from before us and that which comes after. We will see how the *Afikoman* has its biblical fulfillment towards the end of the *Haggadah*.

Stage Five: *Magid* – מגיד (The Telling)

> Stage five is the longest section of the *Haggadah* as it focuses on telling the story of the first Passover while making spiritual application for us today. The telling of the story of Passover in the *Haggadah* begins with a declaration and an invitation to eat the bread of Passover.

(**Leader**: *Hold up the wrapped Afikoman and declare the following statement which begins with the Aramaic phrase*: "**Ha Lachma Anya**" - "**This is the bread of affliction**...")

> **This is the bread of affliction, the poor bread, which our ancestors ate in the land of Egypt. All who are hungry should come and eat. All who are in need should celebrate Passover. Now we are here, next year may we be in the Land of Israel! Now we are slaves, next year may we all be a people who are free!** (A traditional Passover blessing)

(**Leader**: *Place the Afikoman on the table and then continue with the following explanations and Scriptures.*)

This is a fitting introduction to the story of Passover as it presents matzah as a common bread of affliction, a "poor man's bread" that is available to everyone. Whoever you are and whatever your past or present afflictions may be, all are welcome to come and celebrate the Passover: to partake of the foods and to remember the story. This all-inclusive invitation calls to mind the invitation found in the book of Isaiah:

> **"Come, all you who are thirsty, come to the waters; and you who have no money, come, buy and eat! Come, buy wine and milk without money and without cost."** (Is. 55:1 - NIV)

In the New Testament, we also read how Yeshua invited everyone who wanted to come to Him in order to find true rest for one's soul:

> 28 **"Come to Me, all who are weary and burdened, and I will give you rest.** 29 **Take My yoke upon you and learn from Me, for I am gentle and humble in heart, and you will find rest for your souls."** (Matt. 11:28-29 - NASB)

Passover recalls how the people of Israel were slaves set free from the dominion of Pharaoh by the power of God. The Ten Plagues provided an opportunity for everyone in Egypt to choose whether they believed in Pharaoh or in Almighty God. Whoever believed in the Word of God and acted upon it was spared the plague of the firstborn son in their family and was set free from that dominion of darkness. The spiritual message of that first Passover is as true today as it was 3500 years ago.

Hiding The *Afikoman*

(**Leader**: *Hide the wrapped Afikoman somewhere in the room where the Passover Seder is being held. The Afikoman* *will need to be placed somewhere in the room with part of the cloth wrapping being seen from the outside. The search for the Afikoman will take place after the meal at stage eleven. **Note**: The manner of hiding the Afikoman should be appropriate to the age of the children or participants so that they are able to find it.)*

The Four Questions
Ma Nishtanah (Why is it different?)

Leader:

The four questions are included in the *Haggadah* as a way to think about the uniqueness of Passover with a special emphasis on involving the children. At this time, the youngest child (person) sitting at the table (with the ability to read) will ask the four questions. **Note**: Although they are called "**The Four Questions**," it is really one question that is then followed by four distinct differences for the night of Passover.

These four questions have also been set to music and are generally sung in Hebrew. The melody is easily found via the internet for those interested in learning it. Whether the questions are read or sung, they are provided here in three options:

1. Hebrew
2. Transliterated Hebrew
3. English

The child (person) who reads or sings the four questions may do so in whichever language is most comfortable.

(**Participant**: *Read or sing the four questions.*)

Question #1

מַה נִּשְׁתַּנָּה הַלַּיְלָה הַזֶּה מִכָּל הַלֵּילוֹת?
שֶׁבְּכָל הַלֵּילוֹת אָנוּ אוֹכְלִין חָמֵץ וּמַצָּה, הַלַּיְלָה הַזֶּה כֻּלוֹ מַצָּה:

Ma nishtana halaila hazeh mikol haleilot?
Shebichol haleilot anu ochlin chameitz u-matzah.
Halaila hazeh kulo matzah.

Why is this night different from all other nights?
On all other nights we eat leavened bread.
Tonight we only eat matzah.

Question #2

שֶׁבְּכָל הַלֵּילוֹת אָנוּ אוֹכְלִין שְׁאָר יְרָקוֹת, הַלַּיְלָה הַזֶּה מָרוֹר:

Shebichol haleilot anu ochlin shi'ar yirakot haleila
hazeh maror.

On all other nights we eat all kinds of vegetables,
but tonight we eat bitter herbs.

Question #3

שֶׁבְּכָל הַלֵּילוֹת אֵין אָנוּ מַטְבִּילִין אֲפִילוּ פַּעַם אֶחָת,
הַלַּיְלָה הַזֶּה שְׁתֵּי פְעָמִים:
Shebichol haleilot ain anu matbilin afilu pa-am echat.
Halaila hazeh shtei fe-amim.

On all other nights we aren't expected to dip our
vegetables one time. Tonight we dip them twice.

Question #4

שֶׁבְּכָל הַלֵּילוֹת אָנוּ אוֹכְלִין בֵּין יוֹשְׁבִין וּבֵין מְסֻבִּין,
הַלַּיְלָה הַזֶּה כֻּלָּנוּ מְסֻבִּין:

*Shebichol haleilot anu ochlin bein yoshvin uvein
m'subin. Halaila hazeh kulanu m'subin.*

**On all other nights we eat either sitting normally or
reclining. Tonight we recline.**

After the four questions are asked, the story of Passover is explained in response to the four questions. The traditional *Haggadah* uses various Scripture verses and teachings from the rabbis as a way to explain the events of Passover. In this *Haggadah* we will read the account of the first Passover in the book of Exodus, chapter 12.

Leader:

1 **While the Israelites were still in the land of Egypt, the LORD gave the following instructions to Moses and Aaron:** 2 **"From now on, this month will be the first month of the year for you.** 3 **Announce to the whole community of Israel that on the tenth day of this month each family must choose a lamb or a young goat for a sacrifice, one animal for each household.**

4 If a family is too small to eat a whole animal, let them share with another family in the neighborhood. Divide the animal according to the size of each family and how much they can eat. 5 The animal you select must be a one-year-old male, either a sheep or a goat, with no defects.

6 "Take special care of this chosen animal until the evening of the fourteenth day of this first month. Then the whole assembly of the community of Israel must slaughter their lamb or young goat at twilight. 7 They are to take some of the blood and smear it on the sides and top of the doorframes of the houses where they eat the animal. 8 That same night they must roast the meat over a fire and eat it along with bitter salad greens and bread made without yeast. 9 Do not eat any of the meat raw or boiled in water. The whole animal—including the head, legs, and internal organs—must be roasted over a fire. 10 Do not leave any of it until the next morning. Burn whatever is not eaten before morning.

11 "These are your instructions for eating this meal: Be fully dressed, wear your sandals, and carry your walking stick in your hand. Eat the meal with urgency, for this is the LORD's Passover. 12 On that night I will pass through the land of Egypt

and strike down every firstborn son and firstborn male animal in the land of Egypt. I will execute judgment against all the gods of Egypt, for I am the LORD! 13 But the blood on your doorposts will serve as a sign, marking the houses where you are staying. When I see the blood, I will pass over you. This plague of death will not touch you when I strike the land of Egypt.

14 "This is a day to remember. Each year, from generation to generation, you must celebrate it as a special festival to the LORD. This is a law for all time. 15 For seven days the bread you eat must be made without yeast. On the first day of the festival, remove every trace of yeast from your homes. Anyone who eats bread made with yeast during the seven days of the festival will be cut off from the community of Israel. 16 On the first day of the festival and again on the seventh day, all the people must observe an official day for holy assembly. No work of any kind may be done on these days except in the preparation of food.

17 "Celebrate this Festival of Unleavened Bread, for it will remind you that I brought your forces out of the land of Egypt on this very day. This festival will be a permanent law for you; celebrate this day from generation to generation.

18 **The bread you eat must be made without yeast from the evening of the fourteenth day of the first month until the evening of the twenty-first day of that month.** 19 **During those seven days, there must be no trace of yeast in your homes. Anyone who eats anything made with yeast during this week will be cut off from the community of Israel. These regulations apply both to the foreigners living among you and to the native-born Israelites.** 20 **During those days you must not eat anything made with yeast. Wherever you live, eat only bread made without yeast."**

21 **Then Moses called all the elders of Israel together and said to them, "Go, pick out a lamb or young goat for each of your families, and slaughter the Passover animal.** 22 **Drain the blood into a basin. Then take a bundle of hyssop branches and dip it into the blood. Brush the hyssop across the top and sides of the doorframes of your houses. And no one may go out through the door until morning.** 23 **For the LORD will pass through the land to strike down the Egyptians. But when he sees the blood on the top and sides of the doorframe, the LORD will pass over your home. He will not permit his death angel to enter your house and strike you down.**

24 "Remember, these instructions are a permanent law that you and your descendants must observe forever. 25 When you enter the land the LORD has promised to give you, you will continue to observe this ceremony. 26 Then your children will ask, 'What does this ceremony mean?' 27 And you will reply, 'It is the Passover sacrifice to the LORD, for he passed over the houses of the Israelites in Egypt. And though he struck the Egyptians, he spared our families.'" When Moses had finished speaking, all the people bowed down to the ground and worshiped. 28 So the people of Israel did just as the LORD had commanded through Moses and Aaron. (Ex. 12:1-28 - NLT)

Reflection Questions Regarding The First Passover

The following questions are provided to help participants consider the details of the first Passover (Exodus 12) and its significance for us today:

1. In which month was the first Passover observed?
2. On which day of the month was the Passover lamb to be chosen and set apart?
3. On which day and at what time was the

Passover lamb to be slaughtered?
4. What was to be done with the blood of the lamb?
5. How was the lamb to be cooked?
6. Which foods were to be eaten together with the lamb?
7. What was to be done with any leftovers from the roasted lamb?
8. For how many years did God command the Passover to be observed?
9. Why do the Jewish people no longer sacrifice the lamb at Passover?
10. Where in the Bible do we read the clearest prophecy of the Messiah as the sacrificial lamb?

God's Mighty Power at Passover

Leader:

The events surrounding Passover speak of the majesty and power of Almighty God and they continue to speak to us today. The details of Passover found in the Bible help us to remember that we serve the same God as Abraham, Isaac, and Jacob, just as we recall in the following verses in Deuteronomy chapter twenty-six:

> 5 **"You must then say in the presence of the LORD your God, 'My ancestor Jacob was a wandering Aramean who went to live as a foreigner in Egypt. His family arrived few in number, but in Egypt they became a large and mighty nation.** 6 **When the Egyptians oppressed and**

**humiliated us by making us their slaves,
7 we cried out to the LORD, the God of
our ancestors. He heard our cries and
saw our hardship, toil, and oppression.
8 So the LORD brought us out of Egypt
with a strong hand and powerful arm, with
overwhelming terror, and with miraculous
signs and wonders.'"** (Deut. 26:5-8 - NLT)

Remembering The Ten Plagues

Another way we remember the power of God at the first
Passover is through recalling the Ten Plagues against the
Egyptians which culminated in the final plague, death of the
firstborn. The tenth plague was only avoided by obeying the
command of God: to slay the Passover lamb and apply its
blood to the doorway of one's home, thereby preventing the
angel of death from entering.

Instructions For Reducing One's Cup of Joy

<u>Leader</u>:

Everyone at the table should have a full glass of wine. For
each of the Ten Plagues everyone will dip their finger into
their wine glass. Then, shake their finger three times over
their plate letting the wine drip onto the plate. Each plague is
recited three times in unison with each drop of wine as it falls.

This act of reducing the symbolic joy from our cups of wine
(Ps. 104:15) while recalling the Ten Plagues is an act of
mercy as we remember the great suffering of the Egyptians
at that time.

Why do we repeat this act three times for each plague?

In Jewish tradition there is often more than one way to do something, including how we remember the Ten Plagues. For many, the tradition is to let only one drop of wine fall from one's finger and to recite each plague once. However, there is also a tradition of repeating this act three times for each plague in order to recall the three-fold power of God: "...*So the LORD brought us out of Egypt (1) with a strong hand and powerful arm, (2) with overwhelming terror, and (3) with miraculous signs and wonders*..." (Deut. 26:8 - NLT)

The Ten Plagues

(**Leader**: *Invite the participants to read each plague three times together with you in unison as three drops of wine fall from their finger onto the plate. Then continue to read the explanation and sing the song that follows.*)

1. **Blood**
2. **Frogs**
3. **Lice**
4. **Swarms of insects**
5. **Pestilence**
6. **Boils**
7. **Hail**
8. **Locusts**
9. **Darkness**
10. **Death of the firstborn**

God's Abundant Grace – *Daiyehnu*

Leader:

The Hebrew word דינו – *Daiyehnu* (pronounced: **Dai-Yeh-Nu**) means "**It is sufficient for us**" or "**It would have been enough for us.**" It is used here in the context of Passover to emphasize that God went above and beyond in redeeming the children of Israel from slavery in Egypt.

> The following lyrics and chords are the first verse and chorus to a popular Passover song called **Daiyehnu**. If you are not familiar with this song and want to learn the proper melody, you can easily find different recorded examples on the internet by searching: "**Dayenu Passover Song**."

Daiyehnu (A traditional Passover song)

```
C          G7         C          G7
i-lu ho-tzi ho-tzi-a-nu, ho-tzi-a-nu mi-mitz-rai-yim
C    G7   C    G7                   C
ho-tzi-a-nu mi-mitz-rai-yim dai-yeh-nu
C          G7         C          G7
i-lu ho-tzi ho-tzi-a-nu, ho-tzi-a-nu mi-mitz-rai-yim
C    G7   C    G7                   C
ho-tzi-a-nu mi-mitz-rai-yim dai-yeh-nu
```

(Translation: "If He had only brought us out of Egypt, it would have been enough for us")

Chorus:

C   G7   C   G7

dai-dai-yeh-nu, dai-dai-yeh-nu, dai-dai-yeh-nu,

                    C

dai-yeh-nu dai-yeh-nu

(Translation: "It would have been enough for us")

Responsive Reading For *Daiyehnu*:

<u>Leader</u>:

Another way we recall God's gracious acts on behalf of the Israelites is to list the various ways God provided for His people as He brought them out of Egypt into the Holy Land. Many of these divine acts which we read in the Scriptures are recounted in the following responsive reading.

(**<u>Leader & Participants</u>**: *The leader reads the first statement in each line and the participants respond with the phrase* "*Daiyehnu!*")

1. If He had brought us out of Egypt, but not executed judgments against them - *Daiyehnu*
2. If He had executed judgments against them, but not upon their gods - *Daiyehnu*
3. If He had executed judgments against their gods, but not slain their firstborn - *Daiyehnu*
4. If He had slain their firstborn, but not given us their wealth - *Daiyehnu*
5. If He had given us their wealth, but not split the sea for us - *Daiyehnu*
6. If He had split the sea for us, but not led us through it on dry land - *Daiyehnu*
7. If He had led us through it on dry land, but not drowned our oppressors in it - *Daiyehnu*

8. If He had drowned our oppressors in it, but not provided for our needs in the desert for forty years - *Daiyehnu*

9. If He had provided for our needs in the desert for forty years, but not fed us the Manna - *Daiyehnu*

10. If He had fed us the Manna, but not given us the Sabbath - *Daiyehnu*

11. If He had given us the Sabbath, but not brought us before Mount Sinai - *Daiyehnu*

12. If He had brought us before Mount Sinai, but not given us the Torah - *Daiyehnu*

13. If He had given us the Torah, but not brought us into the Land of Israel - *Daiyehnu*

14. If He had brought us into the Land of Israel, but not built the Temple for us - *Daiyehnu*

A Messianic Addition:

15. If He had given us His Son, Yeshua the Messiah, to redeem us from our sin, but had not called us His sons and daughters - *Daiyehnu!*

To Be Called The Children of God

Leader:
Just as the LORD was gracious and generous to the children of Israel in the events surrounding the first Passover, how much more has the Father in heaven been gracious and generous to us by means of the Lamb of God at the final Passover:

> 9 **This was the true Light that, coming into the world, enlightens every person. 10 He was in the world, and the world came into being through Him, and yet the world did not know Him. 11 He came to His own,**

**and His own people did not accept Him.
12 But as many as received Him, to them
He gave the right to become children of
God, to those who believe in His name,
13 who were born, not of blood, nor of the
will of the flesh, nor of the will of a man,
but of God.** (John 1:9-13 - NASB)

God has not only redeemed us from slavery to sin and
cleansed us from our sin by the sacrifice of Yeshua but He
has also given us the privilege to be born again and the right
to become His children. Praise the Lord!

Questions & Answers

(**Leader**: *Read or appoint someone to read the three
questions (Q) followed by the answers (A) which are taken
from Scripture.*)

1. *Pesach* – פסח (The Passover Sacrifice)

(Q) Why did the Israelites continue to eat the Passover
sacrifice up until the Second Temple was destroyed in 70 AD?

(A) **25 "When you enter the land the LORD has
promised to give you, you will continue to
observe this ceremony. 26 Then your children
will ask, 'What does this ceremony mean?' 27
And you will reply, 'It is the Passover sacrifice
to the LORD, for he passed over the houses of
the Israelites in Egypt. And though he struck
the Egyptians, he spared our families.'" When
Moses had finished speaking, all the people
bowed down to the ground and worshiped.**
(Ex. 12:25-27 - NLT)

2. *Matzah* – מצה (Unleavened Bread)

(Q) Why do we eat unleavened bread?

> **(A) And they baked the dough which they had brought out of Egypt into cakes of unleavened bread. For it had no yeast, since they were driven out of Egypt and could not delay, nor had they prepared any provisions for themselves.** (Ex. 12:39 - NASB)

3. *Maror* – מרור (Bitter Herbs)

(Q) Why do we eat bitter herbs?

> **(A) 13 The Egyptians used violence to compel the sons of Israel to labor; 14 and they made their lives bitter with hard labor in mortar and bricks and at all kinds of labor in the field, all their labors which they violently had them perform as slaves.** (Ex. 1:13-14 - NASB)

The above questions and answers are foundational to the Passover Seder as explained by Rabbi Reuven Bulka:

> **These three items, Pesah (the Paschal sacrifice), Matzah (the unleavened bread), and Maror (the bitter herbs), relate to the three purposes of the *Haggadah*, and, as Rabban Gamliel stresses, if they are not meaningfully appreciated, one has not really told the story properly.** (Bulka. P. 80 [Pesah (Pesach) and Paschal are forms of the word Passover])

A Response of Praise

<u>Leader</u>:

We thank God and praise Him for the great deliverance He has provided the Israelites from the land of Egypt, the land of slavery, by reciting the following two psalms. (*Read Psalm 113 & 114 or appoint someone to read them.*)

Psalm 113

1 Praise the LORD! [הללויה – *Hallelu-Yah*]
Praise, O servants of the LORD,
Praise the name of the LORD.
2 Blessed be the name of the LORD
From this time forth and forever.
3 From the rising of the sun to its setting
The name of the LORD is to be praised.
4 The LORD is high above all nations;
His glory is above the heavens.
5 Who is like the LORD our God,
Who is enthroned on high,
6 Who humbles Himself to behold
The things that are in heaven and in the earth?
7 He raises the poor from the dust
And lifts the needy from the ash heap,
8 To make them sit with princes,
With the princes of His people.
9 He makes the barren woman abide in the house as a joyful mother of children.
Praise the LORD! [הללויה – *Hallelu-Yah*]
(NASB1995 – Hebrew added for emphasis)

Psalm 114

1 **When Israel went forth from Egypt,
The house of Jacob from a people of strange language,**
2 **Judah became His sanctuary,
Israel, His dominion.**
3 **The sea looked and fled;
The Jordan turned back.**
4 **The mountains skipped like rams,
The hills, like lambs.**
5 **What ails you, O sea, that you flee?
O Jordan, that you turn back?**
6 **O mountains, that you skip like rams?
O hills, like lambs?**
7 **Tremble, O earth, before the Lord,
Before the God of Jacob,**
8 **Who turned the rock into a pool of water, the flint into a fountain of water.**
(NASB1995)

The following traditional blessing is included in the standard Jewish *Haggadah* and reflects well the heart of the Orthodox Jew who does not yet believe in Yeshua as the Messiah. This particular Jewish blessing is included here to help the reader understand that the Temple and sacrificial system are still a heart's cry of the Jewish people.

A Traditional Jewish Blessing

Leader:

The following is a traditional Jewish blessing:

> **Blessed are You, O LORD our God, King of the universe, Who redeemed us and redeemed our ancestors from Egypt and have brought us to this night that we may eat matzah and maror. Therefore, O LORD our God and God of our fathers, bring us to the Appointed Times and to the other coming Festivals that they may greet us in peace, rejoicing in the rebuilding of Your city and eager in Your service. There we shall eat from the sacrifices and from the Passover offerings whose blood will reach the side of Your altar which will be pleasing. We shall then give thanks to you with a new song regarding our redemption and for the setting free of our souls. Blessed are You, O LORD, Who has redeemed Israel.** (A traditional blessing translated from the Hebrew)

The above blessing is now explained by Rabbi Reuven Bulka to help interpret this blessing and to reveal the heart of Orthodox Judaism:

> **Here we are making our desires for ultimate redemption quite clear. We want this to be the last festival that is celebrated in the constraints of a world without peace, a Yerushalayim (*Jerusalem*) that is**

> **not totally rebuilt, a temple area without a functioning Temple. We yearn for the time that we can "partake from the sacrificial offerings and the Paschal offerings** (*sacrificial lambs at Passover*)**."** (Bulka. p. 91. [words in parentheses added for clarity.])

This blessing and rabbinic commentary clearly reveal the desire in the heart of Orthodox Judaism to realize a rebuilt Temple in Jerusalem with active sacrifices for the sake of blood atonement in this day and age.

The Scriptures tell us there is no forgiveness without the shedding of blood (Lev. 17:11. Heb. 9:22). In general, the human heart knows that all is not right in this world and that there must be a blood sacrifice for sin. Unfortunately, this yearning has been answered in various religions without bringing true forgiveness. This principle of an atoning blood sacrifice is still sought after in Judaism, it is practiced in Islam by means of a yearly animal sacrifice, and it is commonly practiced around the world in many tribal and folk religions (e.g., various sects of Hinduism). A complete and just fulfillment of a blood sacrifice for sin is only found in the Messianic faith, commonly known as Christianity.

Thanks be to God for the sinless blood sacrifice of the Son of God on Passover approximately 2000 years ago. Orthodox Judaism waits in anticipation for a rebuilt Temple in Jerusalem to revive atoning blood sacrifices. We who believe in the death, burial, and resurrection of the Messiah trust in His perfect sacrifice and wait in eager expectation for His Second Coming as He brings salvation to all who know and wait on Him (Heb. 9:23-28).

The Second Cup: The Cup of Deliverance

(**Leader:** *Invite the participants to join in reciting this blessing with you.*)

בָּרוּךְ אַתָּה יהוה אֱלֹהֵינוּ מֶלֶךְ הָעוֹלָם בּוֹרֵא פְּרִי הַגָּפֶן

Baruk Ata Adonai Eloheinu Melek Ha'Olam
Borei Pri Hagafen

Blessed are you, O LORD our God, King of the universe who creates the fruit of the vine.

(**Participants**: *Drink the second cup.*)

Stage Six: *Rachtzah* – רחצה (Washing)

Leader:
The Jewish tradition for this stage, according to the rabbis, is to wash hands before touching the matzah bread in the next stages. We read in the New Testament how Yeshua often debated with the Pharisees regarding the washing of hands as He declared that it was a man-made law and did not come from God in heaven (Matt. 15:1-20).

Washing hands is obviously not an evil practice as each of us does this everyday; however, it is good and necessary to separate what God has commanded from what man has invented as a religious requirement. While understanding a biblical perspective of washing hands, we see in the New Testament a practical act of washing demonstrated by Messiah with His disciples.

At The Last Supper, Yeshua took a basin of water together with a towel and washed His disciples feet (John 13:1-17).

Yeshua did this as an example for His disciples in order to show them how they should serve one another. This principle of serving one another is as important for us today as it was then for all who follow Yeshua as Lord.

Serving One Another

Depending on the situation and the desire of your family or community, you may choose to have everyone participate in a foot washing ceremony or handwashing ceremony as a means of humbling yourselves and serving one another. The focus here is not on specific body parts, hands or feet, but rather on serving one another.

There is no right or wrong way to handle this stage of the Passover Seder and there should be freedom to express it in a non-legalistic manner. The handwashing ceremony, as outlined below, is included as a way to integrate the Jewish tradition at this stage of the Passover Seder together with a fulfillment of Yeshua's example of serving His disciples.

Preparation for
The Handwashing Ceremony

Items needed for the handwashing ceremony:
1. Plastic bowl (medium to large-sized for catching water)
2. Hand towel

3. Pitcher of water
4. Scriptures (provided below)

A Step-by-Step Explanation: The empty bowl should be placed in front of the person on either side of the leader at the table. That person should extend their hands over the empty bowl as the leader pours a bit of water from the pitcher over their hands. The leader will then offer the hand towel in order to dry their hands. The person with the washed hands will then serve the next person in a similar manner until everyone around the table has washed their hands.

In completing this handwashing ceremony, we practice the command of Yeshua to serve one another as He instructed His disciples.

The Handwashing Ceremony

(**Leader & Participants**: *The leader should read or appoint someone to read John 13 as the participants around the table serve one another in this handwashing ceremony.*)

5 **Then He poured water into the basin, and began to wash the disciples' feet and to wipe them with the towel with which He was girded. 6 So He came to Simon Peter. He said to Him, "Lord, do You wash my feet?" 7** *Yeshua* **answered and said to him, "What I do you do not realize now,**

but you will understand hereafter." 8 Peter said to Him, "Never shall You wash my feet!" *Yeshua* answered him, "If I do not wash you, you have no part with Me." 9 Simon Peter said to Him, "Lord, then wash not only my feet, but also my hands and my head." 10 *Yeshua* said to him, "He who has bathed needs only to wash his feet, but is completely clean; and you are clean, but not all of you." 11 For He knew the one who was betraying Him; for this reason He said, "Not all of you are clean." 12 So when He had washed their feet, and taken His garments and reclined at the table again, He said to them, "Do you know what I have done to you? 13 You call Me Teacher and Lord; and you are right, for so I am. 14 If I then, the Lord and the Teacher, washed your feet, you also ought to wash one another's feet. 15 For I gave you an example that you also should do as I did to you. 16 Truly, truly, I say to you, a slave is not greater than his master, nor is one who is sent greater than the one who sent him. 17 If you know these things, you are blessed if you do them." (John 13:5-17 - NASB1995)

We do not have to serve one another by means of some formal act; however, as Yeshua stated, we are "blessed" if we do!

Stage Seven: *Motzi* – מוציא
(To Bring Forth)

Leader:

The following blessing on matzah is a traditional blessing that is said over bread whenever bread in any form (leavened or unleavened) is eaten. At Passover, this blessing is said over matzah in general and then a separate blessing is specifically recited over the three matzahs in the matzah bag, including the middle piece which is broken in half. (**Note**: there is no eating of matzah associated with the blessing of stage seven.)

(**Leader**: *Hold up all three matzahs in the matzah bag while reading the following blessing. Invite participants to join in reciting this blessing with you.*)

בָּרוּךְ אַתָּה יהוה אֱלֹהֵינוּ מֶלֶךְ הָעוֹלָם הַמוֹצִיא
לֶחֶם מִן־הָאָרֶץ:

***Baruk Ata Adonai Eloheinu Melek Ha'olam Hamotzi
Lechem Min Ha'Aretz***

**Blessed are you, O LORD our God, King of the universe
who brings forth bread from the earth.**

Stage Eight: *Matzah* – מצה (Unleavened Bread)

(**Leader:** *Take out the top and middle half-piece of matzah from the matzah bag. Set the bottom matzah aside and read the following blessing over the top two matzahs: the full top and middle half-piece. Invite participants to join in reciting this blessing with you.*)

בָּרוּךְ אַתָּה יהוה אֱלֹהֵינוּ מֶלֶךְ הָעוֹלָם
אֲשֶׁר קִדְּשָׁנוּ בְּיֵשׁוּעַ הַמָּשִׁיחַ וְצִוָּנוּ עַל־אֲכִילַת מַצָּה:

*Baruk Ata Adonai Eloheinu Melek Ha'olam
Asher Kidshanu Be'Yeshua HaMashiach VeTzivanu
Al Ahilat Matzah*

Blessed are you, O LORD our God, King of the universe who sanctified us in Yeshua the Messiah and commanded us to eat matzah.

(**Leader**: *Break the one and a half matzahs into bite-sized pieces and put them on a plate to be distributed to everyone at the table. If there is not enough matzah from the one and a half pieces for all of those at your table, then extra matzah may be added.*)

(**Participants**: *Each one should receive a piece of matzah and eat it.*)

Stage Nine: *Maror* – מרור (Bitter Herbs)

(**Participants**: *Take a piece of romaine lettuce and put some Charoset [sweet apple mixture] on it together with some horseradish.*)

> The **romaine lettuce** is considered a **bitter herb**; however, it is not so bitter. Therefore, we add some horseradish to experience the pain of slavery in a more pungent manner. The ***Charoset*** (literally potter's clay) represents the Jewish people. By eating the bitter herbs together with the sweet apple mixture we remember how our ancestors experienced the pain of slavery in Egypt.

(**Leader**: *Read the following blessing and invite the participants to join in reciting this blessing with you.*)

בָּרוּךְ אַתָּה יהוה אֱלֹהֵינוּ מֶלֶךְ הָעוֹלָם
אֲשֶׁר קִדְּשָׁנוּ בְּיֵשׁוּעַ הַמָּשִׁיחַ וְצִוָּנוּ עַל־אֲכִילַת מָרוֹר:

**Baruk Ata Adonai Eloheinu Melek Ha'olam
Asher Kidshanu Be'Yeshua HaMashiach VeTzivanu
Al Ahilat Maror**

Blessed are you, O LORD our God, King of the universe who sanctified us in Yeshua the Messiah and commanded us to eat bitter herbs.

(**Participants**: *This unique combination of lettuce, horseradish, and the sweet apple-cinnamon mixture is now eaten.*)

Stage Ten: *Korech* – כורך (Sandwich)

> The sandwich stage is an opportunity to eat the traditional foods of Passover in any combination between two pieces of matzah, thereby making a sandwich. There is no blessing for this stage and everyone is free to make a sandwich as explained below.

(**Leader**: *Take the bottom whole piece of matzah from the matzah bag and break it into bite-sized pieces. Share these pieces with all participants.*)

(**Participants**: *Make a sandwich using any combination of Passover foods on the table including the romaine lettuce, the apple mixture, and the horseradish.*)

Stage Eleven: *Shulchan Orek* – שולחן עורך (The Set Table)

> It is now time for dinner. Sufficient time should be given for everyone to eat the main meal, including dessert. According to Jewish tradition, the only remaining food to be eaten after the main meal is the *Afikoman*. After everyone is finished with the main meal, the Passover Seder continues with the final four stages of the *Haggadah*.

(Interlude For The Main Meal & Dessert)

Stage Twelve: *Tzafoon* – צפון (Hidden)

> The Hebrew word צפון (*Tzafoon*) means **hidden** or **concealed**. It is at this stage in the Passover Seder that a search is made for the broken piece of matzah which was hidden away at the beginning of the Seder: the *Afikoman*. The search should be completed before moving forward.

(**Leader**: *Invite all of the children [generally those 17 years old and younger or the youngest members at the table] to search for the Afikoman which was hidden earlier somewhere in the room.*)

(**Participants**: *The one who finds the Afikoman will then bring it to the leader who purchases or redeems the Afikoman from whoever finds it.*)

> The redemption price for the *Afikoman* is generally a small sum of money (e.g., 20 shekels, $5, or €5) or a gift of some sort (e.g., a chocolate bar) that is made ready ahead of time. The act of redeeming the *Afikoman* is to remind us of the importance of this piece of matzah which has come to represent the Passover lamb.

(**Leader**: *Read the following paragraphs which further explain the meaning of the Afikoman and its connection to The Communion Service.*)

Leader:
The First Temple (of Solomon) was destroyed in 586 BC and the Second Temple, which was built by the Jewish exiles who returned to Jerusalem and later renovated by King Herod, was destroyed in 70 AD. As a result of no standing Temple in Jerusalem today nor an altar on which to sacrifice the Passover lamb, the *Afikoman* is used to symbolize the Passover lamb.

The Importance of The *Afikoman*

Leader:
The *Afikoman* is the last piece of food eaten on the night of Passover and it should linger in our mouths to remind us of the sacrificial lamb. Rabbi Bulka confirms this ancient Jewish tradition:

> **The *Afikoman*, or last food, is a piece of Matzah. This piece of Matzah is designed to be a reminder of the Paschal** *(Passover)* **sacrifice and is the taste with which we leave the Seder**. (Bulka. p.24. [words in parentheses added for clarity])

The elevating of this seemingly insignificant piece of matzah, the *Afikoman*, to the place of representing the sacrificial Passover lamb cannot be overstated. According to Jewish tradition, the stages of the *Haggadah* following the main meal, beginning with the *Afikoman*, shift from focusing on the past redemption from Egypt 3500 years ago to the future Messianic redemption. We will now see how Jewish

tradition and the New Testament merge together for a divine fulfillment.

The *Afikoman* in The New Testament

Leader:

It stands to reason that the *Afikoman* is the same piece of matzah that Yeshua used at the Passover of The Last Supper to identify with His body. We will see how the *Afikoman* and other traditions from the Passover Seder are the foundation for establishing The New Covenant and the symbols for what we know today as the elements of The Communion Service.

It is at this time in the Passover Seder that all the steps of Communion will be observed in their natural order as we go through the *Haggadah*. The precise order we follow in the Passover Seder may be a bit different from what we are familiar with in our weekly or monthly service with our local congregation; however, this should not distract us from the deeper meaning in this ancient practice. The goal is to understand the source of what Yeshua instituted at the Passover 2000 years ago (The New Covenant) and to see how He and His disciples followed many of the same customs and practices that Orthodox Jews still follow today in the Passover Seder.

This unique Communion observation will not only help us better understand the foundations of The Communion Service, but also demonstrates how Yeshua's life and death perfectly fulfill the biblical Passover.

We will read the fuller context of The Last Supper in the Gospels later in the *Haggadah*; however, for now we will follow the instructions in 1 Corinthians 11 as we partake of The Lord's Supper.

Passover & The Communion Service

Leader:
We will now partake of The Communion Service. Since this piece of Matzah represents the body of Messiah, it is recommended that only believers in Yeshua as the Messiah participate in this part of the Seder. (*Take the Afikoman, hold it up, and read the following Scripture.*):

> **23 For I received from the Lord that which I also delivered to you, that the Lord *Yeshua* in the night in which He was betrayed took bread; 24 and when He had given thanks, He broke it and said, "This is My body, which is for you; do this in remembrance of Me."** (1 Cor. 11:23-24 - NASB1995)

(**Leader**: *The Afikoman is to be broken into bite-sized pieces and passed around to each person at the table. The leader then continues to read.*)

As we eat this matzah bread we remember the broken body of our Messiah which was given for our redemption from sin and death.

(**Participants**: *Everyone now eats a piece of the Afikoman remembering the broken body of Messiah.*)

Leader:
As we eat this piece of matzah, we recall that the *Afikoman* is a part of the three matzahs in the matzah bag with evident symbolism to the trinity: The Father, The Son, and The Holy Spirit. Just as the middle piece is taken out, broken, hidden away for a time, and then later brought back to the

table, so too Yeshua the Messiah was broken through His death on the cross, hidden away in the grave for a time, and resurrected to life on the third day.

The biblical commandments of Passover and the Jewish traditions continue to speak of the Messiah's sinless life in the unleavened bread which is striped and pierced through, broken in half, and later redeemed to give us the complete picture of our redemption from sin at the Passover.

Stage Thirteen: *Barek* – ברך (Blessing)

<u>Leader</u>:
Before we drink the third cup of wine, which is part of the traditional Communion service, we take a few minutes to give thanks to God for the food we have eaten throughout the Passover Seder.

The thirteenth stage is a time of giving thanks after the meal in keeping with the exhortation in Deuteronomy chapter eight:

> **When you have eaten and are satisfied,**
> **you shall bless the LORD your God for**
> **the good land which He has given you.**
> (Deut. 8:10 - NASB1995)

Saying a blessing after the meal is a tradition that is regularly practiced in everyday Jewish life. It is always good to give thanks to God for the many blessings He has given us, including the daily food we eat.

There is no specific way to give thanks to God, and it is good to be creative with this stage of "blessing." The leader may give

thanks to God on behalf of everyone present or those sitting at the table can be given an opportunity to give thanks to God recalling His many blessings, including the food that has been eaten.

The traditional Jewish practice of giving thanks after the meal begins with reciting or singing Psalm 126 and then continues in a prayer of praise and thanksgiving.

(**Leader**: *Read Psalm 126 and then continue with a prayer of thanksgiving.*)

Psalm 126: A Song of Ascents

1 **When the LORD brought back the captives of Zion,**
We were like those who dream.
2 **Then our mouth was filled with laughter**
And our tongue with joyful shouting;
Then they said among the nations,
"The LORD has done great things for them."
3 **The LORD has done great things for us; we are joyful.**
4 **Restore our fortunes, LORD, as the streams in the South.**
5 **Those who sow in tears shall harvest with joyful shouting.**
6 **One who goes here and there weeping, carrying his bag of seed,**

Shall indeed come again with a shout of joy, bringing his sheaves with him. (NASB)

(**Participants**: *After the time of blessing and giving thanks, everyone around the table should check to make sure their glasses are filled in preparation for the third cup of wine.*)

The Third Cup: The Cup of Redemption

<u>Leader</u>:

We will now continue with the third cup of wine and drink it after reciting the blessing together. The third cup of wine falls between stages thirteen and fourteen of the *Haggadah* and seems to have minor significance in the Passover Seder; however, it is this cup of wine that parallels the cup that Yeshua took during The Last Supper when He instituted The New Covenant.

The third cup is the one that comes after the meal and is also called "The Cup of Redemption." When Yeshua took this cup during the Passover Seder 2000 years ago He stated that this cup is The New Covenant in His blood. He also declared that by His blood He would redeem humanity from slavery to sin and provide redemption for all who would believe in Him. The Apostle Paul speaks of this third cup in his instructions regarding The Communion Service in his letter to the Corinthian believers:

> 25 **In the same way He took the cup also after supper, saying, "This cup is the new covenant in My blood; do this, as often as you drink it, in remembrance of Me." 26 For as often as you eat this bread and**

drink the cup, you proclaim the Lord's death until He comes. (1 Cor. 11:25-26 - NASB1995)

(**Leader**: *Before drinking the third cup, invite participants to join in the traditional blessing for the third cup of wine.*):

בָּרוּךְ אַתָּה יהוה אֱלֹהֵינוּ מֶלֶךְ הָעוֹלָם בּוֹרֵא פְּרִי הַגָּפֶן:

Baruk Ata Adonai Eloheinu Melek Ha'Olam Borei Pri Hagafen

Blessed are you, O LORD our God, King of the universe who creates the fruit of the vine.

Leader:
Everyone who believes in Yeshua as the Messiah is now free to drink The Cup of Redemption as we remember how our Messiah used this cup to institute The New Covenant in His blood.

(**Participants**: *After drinking the third cup, everyone's glass should be filled one more time in preparation for the fourth cup.*)

The Coming of Elijah

Leader:
The Passover Seder not only remembers the past redemption at the first Passover 3500 years ago, but it also looks forward to the future Messianic redemption that is still to come. The Scriptures prophesy that Elijah the prophet will be sent before "**the great and terrible day of the LORD**," which is considered to be a Messianic prophecy related to the End Times. Jewish tradition includes a segment of the *Haggadah*

with the expectant hope that Elijah the prophet will come soon in order that we may see the coming of Messiah. This Messianic prophecy is found in the book of Malachi:

> **Behold, I am going to send you Elijah the prophet before the coming of the great and terrible day of the LORD**. (Malachi 4:5 - NASB1995)

In a practical and tangible manner, Jewish tradition includes a step of literally checking the door to see if Elijah has come and will take his seat at the Passover table. This is a symbolic gesture; however, it is done in the hope of Messiah's Coming.

(**Leader**: *Ask or appoint one of the children, or an adult if no child present, to open the door to see if Elijah is there.*)

Leader:
We know from New Testament Scriptures that this same expectation of Elijah's coming was clearly known and taught among the Jewish people of Yeshua's day. In the Gospel of Matthew we read the following dialogue which occurred after the events on the Mount of Transfiguration:

> 9 **As they were coming down from the mountain, *Yeshua* commanded them, saying, "Tell the vision to no one until the Son of Man has risen from the dead."** 10 **And His disciples asked Him, "Why then do the scribes say that Elijah must come first?"** 11 **And He answered and said, "Elijah is coming and will restore all things;** 12 **but I say to you that Elijah already came, and they did not recognize him, but did to him whatever they wished.**

So also the Son of Man is going to suffer at their hands." 13 Then the disciples understood that He had spoken to them about John the Baptist. (Matt. 17:9-13 - NASB1995)

Questions For Discussion

Has Elijah already come or is he still to come before Messiah's Second Coming?

We read how Yeshua explained in Matthew 17:9-13 that John the Baptist came in the spirit and power of Elijah 2000 years ago; however, Yeshua also said that Elijah is coming and will restore all things. Yeshua spoke of a past fulfillment of the Elijah prophecy through John the Baptist and yet He also spoke of a future coming of Elijah in regard to this same prophecy.

Therefore, in what manner will Elijah come in the future and "restore all things"?

Stage Fourteen: *Hallel* – הלל (Praise)

Leader:

As we approach the end of the *Haggadah*, stage fourteen focuses on giving praise to the Lord. We will fulfill this stage by reading a couple of different psalms. But first, we will connect The Communion Service to Passover and put all of the pieces together.

We have already seen a direct fulfillment of both the *Afikoman* and the third cup of wine in the Passover Seder through Yeshua's body and blood in the institution of The New Covenant. **What about this fourteenth stage of *Hallel* (praise)? Is there a fulfillment of this act of praise during the Passover of The Last Supper?**

The Last Supper

Leader:

We find answers to the above questions as we read the account of The Last Supper in the Gospel of Matthew:

> 26 **While they were eating, *Yeshua* took some bread, and after a blessing, He broke it and gave it to the disciples, and said, "Take, eat; this is My body."** 27 **And when He had taken a cup and given thanks, He gave it to them, saying, "Drink from it, all of you;** 28 **for this is My blood of the covenant, which is poured out for many for forgiveness of sins.** 29 **But I say to you, I will not drink of this fruit of the vine from now on until that day when I drink it new with you in My Father's**

kingdom." 30 After singing a hymn, they went out to the Mount of Olives. (Matt. 26:26-30 - NASB1995)

Connections & Conclusions:

- Yeshua took a piece of unleavened bread, which we know today as the *Afikoman*, and shared it with His disciples to represent His body.
- Yeshua took the third cup of wine after the meal, The Cup of Redemption, to represent His blood of The New Covenant.
- Before leaving the Passover table, Yeshua and His disciples praised God by singing a hymn and then went to the Mount of Olives.

The Passover Seder that traditional Jews still observe today aligns well with what we read in the New Testament when Yeshua observed the Passover with His disciples 2000 years ago, including this stage of praise (*Hallel*) at the end of the Passover Seder.

The accuracy of the many details in the Passover Seder today and how they align with the record of the New Testament and the life of Yeshua is a powerful testimony in itself. The alignment of these details should greatly encourage every believer's faith as we see God's Word fulfilled. The many pieces to this spiritual puzzle of God's redemptive plan through the Messiah, from Genesis to Revelation, are a clear and bold testimony to Jew and Gentile alike.

A Night of Keeping Watch

In Exodus chapter twelve we read how the day of Passover was uniquely set apart on God's calendar:

> 41 **And at the end of four hundred and thirty years, to the very day, all the hosts of the LORD went out from the land of Egypt.** 42 **It is a night to be observed for the LORD for having brought them out from the land of Egypt; this night is for the LORD, to be observed by all the sons of Israel throughout their generations.** (Ex. 12:41-42 - NASB1995)

More than 500 years earlier, the LORD had spoken prophetically to Abraham that his descendants would be enslaved in a foreign land for 400 years. This was fulfilled exactly as God had foretold it (Gen. 15:12-14).

We also read in Exodus 12:42 that the night of Passover was to be set apart as a special night to the LORD. The first phrase of verse 42 in Hebrew reads as follows:

לֵיל שִׁמֻרִים הוּא לַיהוָה

... Lel Shimorim Hu L'Adonai

It is a night to be observed for the LORD..." or "It is a night of keeping watch for the LORD..."

This unique form of the Hebrew word לשמור – *Lishmor* (to watch, to observe, to keep) as שימורים - *Shimorim* only appears once in all of the Bible.

- **In what way is the night of Passover "to be observed for the LORD"?**

- **How do we see a prophetic fulfillment of the night of Passover as "...a night of keeping watch for the LORD"?**

Praise – *Hallel*

<u>Leader</u>:

Psalm 117

1 Praise the LORD, all you nations.
Praise him, all you people of the earth.
2 For his unfailing love for us is powerful;
The LORD's faithfulness endures forever.
Praise the LORD! (NLT)

(<u>**Leader & Participants**</u>: *The leader reads the first line of each verse as participants respond with the repeated phrase "**For His lovingkindness is everlasting**" or with the Hebrew phrase:* כִּי לְעוֹלָם חַסְדּוֹ - "**Ki LeOlam Chasdo.**")

Psalm 136

1 Give thanks to the LORD, for He is good,
For His lovingkindness is everlasting.
(*Ki LeOlam Chasdo*)

2 Give thanks to the God of gods,
For His lovingkindness is everlasting.
(*Ki LeOlam Chasdo*)

3 Give thanks to the Lord of lords,
For His lovingkindness is everlasting.
(*Ki LeOlam Chasdo*)

4 To Him who alone does great wonders,
For His lovingkindness is everlasting.
(*Ki LeOlam Chasdo*)

5 To Him who made the heavens with skill,
For His lovingkindness is everlasting.
(*Ki LeOlam Chasdo*)

6 To Him who spread out the earth above the waters,
For His lovingkindness is everlasting.
(*Ki LeOlam Chasdo*)

7 To Him who made the great lights,
For His lovingkindness is everlasting.
(*Ki LeOlam Chasdo*)

8 The sun to rule by day,
For His lovingkindness is everlasting.
(*Ki LeOlam Chasdo*)

9 The moon and stars to rule by night,
For His lovingkindness is everlasting.
(*Ki LeOlam Chasdo*)

10 To Him who smote the Egyptians in their firstborn,
For His lovingkindness is everlasting.
(*Ki LeOlam Chasdo*)

11 And brought Israel out from their midst,
For His lovingkindness is everlasting.
(*Ki LeOlam Chasdo*)

12 With a strong hand and an outstretched arm,
For His lovingkindness is everlasting.
(*Ki LeOlam Chasdo*)

13 To Him who divided the Red Sea asunder,
For His lovingkindness is everlasting.
(*Ki LeOlam Chasdo*)

14 And made Israel pass through the midst of it,
For His lovingkindness is everlasting.
(*Ki LeOlam Chasdo*)

15 But He overthrew Pharaoh and his army in the Red Sea,
For His lovingkindness is everlasting.
(*Ki LeOlam Chasdo*)

16 To Him who led His people through the wilderness,
For His lovingkindness is everlasting.
(*Ki LeOlam Chasdo*)

17 To Him who smote great kings,
For His lovingkindness is everlasting.
(*Ki LeOlam Chasdo*)

18 And slew mighty kings,
For His lovingkindness is everlasting.
(*Ki LeOlam Chasdo*)

19 Sihon, king of the Amorites,
For His lovingkindness is everlasting.
(*Ki LeOlam Chasdo*)

20 And Og, king of Bashan,
For His lovingkindness is everlasting.
(*Ki LeOlam Chasdo*)

21 And gave their land as a heritage,
For His lovingkindness is everlasting.
(*Ki LeOlam Chasdo*)

22 Even a heritage to Israel His servant,
For His lovingkindness is everlasting.
(*Ki LeOlam Chasdo*)

23 Who remembered us in our low estate,
For His lovingkindness is everlasting.
(*Ki LeOlam Chasdo*)

24 And has rescued us from our adversaries,
For His lovingkindness is everlasting.
(*Ki LeOlam Chasdo*)

25 Who gives food to all flesh,
For His lovingkindness is everlasting.
(*Ki LeOlam Chasdo*)

26 Give thanks to the God of heaven,
For His lovingkindness is everlasting.
(*Ki LeOlam Chasdo*)

(NASB1995)

The Fourth Cup: The Cup of Praise
Leader:
The fourth cup of wine is the final cup of the Passover Seder and looks to a future, global redemption when all nations of the earth will truly praise the Lord (Is. 2:1-4). This cup of praise looks forward to the ultimate redemption when the Messiah comes to reign on earth (Zech. 14:9).

Before we drink this final cup, we recite together the traditional blessing for wine:

בָּרוּךְ אַתָּה יהוה אֱלֹהֵינוּ מֶלֶךְ הָעוֹלָם בּוֹרֵא פְּרִי הַגָּפֶן:

***Baruk Ata Adonai Eloheinu Melek Ha'Olam
Borei Pri Hagafen***

Blessed are you, O LORD our God, King of the universe who creates the fruit of the vine.

(**Participants**: *Everyone drinks the fourth cup.*)

Discussion Questions: The Four Cups of Wine & The *Afikoman*

1. Did Yeshua and His disciples drink this fourth cup?

It is difficult to know the answer to this question with certainty; however, it seems they did not drink the fourth cup at that time. In Matthew's account of The Last Supper, we read again Yeshua's words after they drank the third cup:

> 29 **"But I say to you, I will not drink of this fruit of the vine from now on until that day when I drink it new with you in My Father's kingdom."** 30 **After singing a hymn, they went out to the Mount of Olives**. (Matt. 26:29-30 - NASB1995)

We do not want to make an argument from silence; however, it seems from these verses

that Yeshua did not drink the last traditional cup of wine after He shared the third cup of redemption with His disciples. As the fourth cup looks forward to the ultimate redemption when the Kingdom of God is established on earth, it seems fitting that Yeshua did not drink the fourth cup at that time. The fourth cup will be part of the celebration after the Second Coming of Messiah.

2. **What is the origin of the four cups of wine and the *Afikoman* (the final piece of matzah)?**

Nowhere in the Bible did God command four cups of wine to be part of the Passover observance. In fact, God did not even command one cup of wine to be part of Passover. The four cups of wine were added as part of Jewish tradition. It is the same for the *Afikoman*. These traditions were added to help tell the story of Passover as well as to emphasize and symbolize the powerful redemption of God on behalf of His people.

Without getting into the various reasons and theories regarding the four cups of wine and the *Afikoman*, we see how these traditional elements were used by God in the Passover celebration 2000 years ago in order to institute The New Covenant.

Stage Fifteen: *Nirtzah* – נרצה (Accepted)

Leader:

We have now come to the final stage of the *Haggadah* and the final blessing of the Passover Seder. This final stage conveys the meaning that we have completed everything necessary to remember the past redemption that was performed by Almighty God at the first Passover, and we look forward to the future redemption that He has planned for us, as well.

For the Jews who lived outside of Jerusalem for nearly 1900 years, it has always been the heart's cry to return to the Holy Land and especially to ascend to the Holy City. In 1948 Israel was reestablished as a nation and Jews have been returning to the Holy Land and celebrating Passover in Jerusalem for more than 75 years. We now end the Passover Seder with that same desire to celebrate Passover "**Next Year in Jerusalem!**"

This heart's cry is not simply a reference for ascending to worship in Jerusalem but also carries with it the future hope of the Messianic era when Messiah will come and establish God's Kingdom on earth. It is with this hope and expectation in mind that we can all now proclaim the following:

(**Leader & Participants**: *All declare in unison*)

לְשָׁנָה הַבָּאָה בִּירוּשָׁלָיִם:

LeShana Haba'ah BiYerushalayim

Next Year in Jerusalem!

This is the conclusion to the Passover Seder!

The Passover Seder is now complete. We at **Ner LeRaglai Jewish Ministries** hope you have enjoyed this unique biblical feast. Our prayer is that you have gained a greater appreciation for the context of The Last Supper and how the Passover celebration still points to Yeshua. If you have found this Messianic Passover Seder experience to be beneficial for you and your family or community, consider organizing a Passover Seder for others next year.

To order more Passover *Hagaddah* books or to invite Daniel Goldstein to lead a Passover Seder, email us at:

admin@nerleraglai.com

Ner LeRaglai Jewish Ministries is a 501c-3 non-profit organization registered in TX, USA. To support this ministry, please go to our website and click the "**Give**" tab at:

www.NerLeRaglai.com

Bibliography:

1. Bulka, Rabbi Reuven P. The Haggadah for Pesah. Machon Pri Ha'Aretz Pub. Jerusalem, Israel. 1985

2. Holy Bible, New International Version. NIV Copyright ©1973, 1978, 1984, 2011 by Biblica, Inc. (NIV)

3. Lau, Rabbi Israel Meir. Practical Judaism. Modan Publishing House Ltd. Tel Aviv, Israel. 1997

4. New American Standard Bible. Copyright © 1960, 1971, 1977, 1995 by The Lockman Foundation. (NASB1995)

5. New American Standard Bible. Copyright © 1960, 1971, 1977, 1995, 2020 by The Lockman Foundation. (NASB)

6. The Holy Bible, New Living Translation. Copyright © 1996, 2004, 2015 by Tyndale House Foundation. Carol Stream, Illinois (NLT)

Made in the USA
Las Vegas, NV
17 April 2024